Men-at-Arms • 367

Medieval Russian Armies 1250–1500

V Shpakovsky & D Nicolle • Illustrated by A McBride

Series editor Martin Windrow

First published in Great Britain in 2002 by Osprey Publishing,
Midland House, West Way, Botley, Oxford OX2 0PH, UK
443 Park Avenue South, New York, NY 10016, USA
Email: info@ospreypublishing.com

© 2002 Osprey Publishing Ltd.
Reprinted 2006

CIP Data for this publication is available from the British Library

ISBN 1 84176 234 2

Editor: Martin Windrow
Design: Alan Hamp
Index by Alan Rutter
Maps by David Nicolle
Originated by Magnet Harlequin, Uxbridge, UK
Printed in China through World Print Ltd.

FOR A CATALOGUE OF ALL BOOKS PUBLISHED BY
OSPREY MILITARY AND AVIATION PLEASE CONTACT:

NORTH AMERICA
Osprey Direct, C/o Random House Distribution Center,
400 Hahn Road, Westminster, MD 21157, USA
E-mail: info@ospreydirect.com

ALL OTHER REGIONS
Osprey Direct UK, P.O. Box 140, Wellingborough,
Northants, NN8 2FA, UK
E-mail: info@ospreydirect.co.uk

www.ospreypublishing.com

Acknowledgements

With special thanks to L.J.Shkolnik, I.Tsipina and A.Triakina for
translating Russian texts; to A.S.Sheps for his artwork of arms and
armour, and O.V.Tymkina for her artwork of timber fortresses.

Artist's Note

OPPOSITE **From the 15th-century copy of the lost
13th-century Radzilovskaya Chronicle, two drawings of
warriors dressed in very different styles. One wears a
garment coming down to just above the knee, the other
an ankle-length robe under his armour; note, however,
that both have the tall, pointed helmets with aventails
which are so characteristic of the Russian tradition.**

MEDIEVAL RUSSIAN ARMIES
1250–1500

THE MONGOL CONQUEST OF RUSSIA

IN 1237 THE MONGOLS INVADED the Russian principality of Ryazan. Three years later the north-western and southern parts of the country lay in ruins. As the invaders made their way across various wealthy Russian principalities, they overcame fortified towns and efficient armies. Russian armies found themselves greatly outnumbered on the field of battle, and there was no unity of purpose among the Russian princes. In the past they had fought wars of feudal rivalry but now, for the first time, the Mongol hordes introduced a new kind of warfare based upon the total destruction of an enemy nation and its culture. In fact it was virtually impossible for any 13th-century European to grasp the scale of the catastrophe, and to understand how his native country and its towns had collapsed. Meanwhile Russia was occupied by the Mongols, forced to pay tribute, and in many areas depopulated, after which the Mongols swarmed on to ravage Eastern Europe.

The scope of this disaster is confirmed by archaeological research, and it is generally agreed that the Mongol invasion held back the development of Russia for up to two centuries. The invasion also had an impact upon the military arts in medieval Russia, although relatively little is known about the military history of Russia from the 13th to the 15th century, which is represented as something of a 'dark age'.

CHRONOLOGY

1259–63	Rule of Prince Alexandr Yaroslavich Nevskii of Vladimir as Grand Prince of Russia.
1276–1303	Rule of Prince Daniil Alexandrovich of Moscow.
1300	Metropolitan Maxim of the Russian Orthodox Church moves from Kiev to Vladimir.
1301	Town of Kolomna annexed by Moscow.
1302	Principality of Pereyaslavl taken over by Moscow.
1303–25	Rule of Prince Yury Danilovich in Moscow.
1316–41	Rule of Prince Gediminas of 'Great Lithuania'.
1318–22	Rule of Yury Danilovich as Grand Prince.
1318	Army of Novgorod destroys Swedish-held Abo in Finland.
1326	Metropolitan Peter of the Russian Orthodox Church moves from Vladimir to Moscow; Moscow becomes the religious centre of Russia.
1327	Russian rebellion against tribute collectors of the Mongol Golden Horde.
1328–41	Rule of Prince Ivan Kalita in Moscow as Grand Prince.

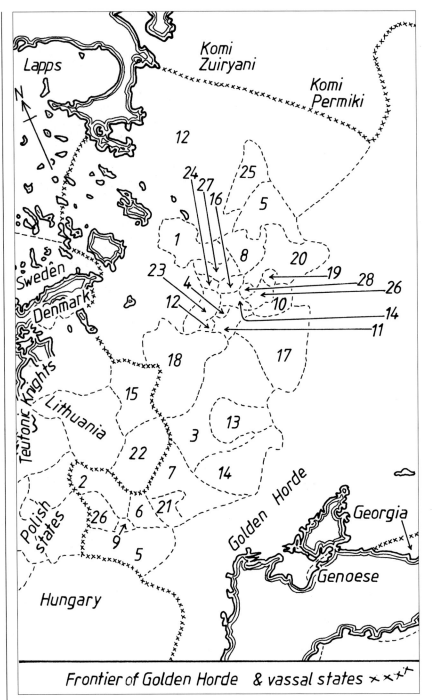

Russian states, c.1270. Note that Polotsk (15) and Turov-Pinsk (22) were the only Russian principalities which did not recognise the overlordship of the Mongol Golden Horde:

(1) Beloozero
(2) Berestie
(3) Chernigov
(4) Dmitrov
(5) Galich
(6) Isyaslavl
(7) Kiev
(8) Kostroma
(9) Kremenets
(10) Murom
(11) Muscovy
(12) Novgorod
(13) Novgorod Seversk
(14) Pereyaslavl
(15) Polotsk
(16) Rostov
(17) Ryazan
(18) Smolensk
(19) Starodub
(20) Suzdal Nizhegorod
(21) Svizhden
(22) Turov-Pinsk
(23) Tver
(24) Uglich
(25) Veliki Ustyug
(26) Vladimir
(27) Yaroslavl,
(28) Yuriev

Frontier of Golden Horde & vassal states ×××⁺

1341–51	Rule of Simeon the Proud as Grand Prince.
1345–77	Rule of Prince Olgerd of 'Great Lithuania' and the western Russian principalities.
1349	Poland annexes Russian territory of Galich.
1353–59	Rule of Grand Prince Ivan Ivanovich the Merciful.
1359–89	Rule of Prince Dmitrii Ivanovich Donskoi in Moscow, recognised by the Mongol Golden Horde as Grand Prince in 1362.
1367–8	Building of the first stone Kremlin (Citadel) in Moscow.

4

OPPOSITE **Asiatic troops attacking a city, probably representing Jerusalem or Constantinople, in the** *Chronicle of Georgi Amartola,* **Russian, 1318–1327. (Lenin Library, Moscow)**

1371	Army of Moscow defeats Prince Oleg of Ryazan.
1377	Jagiello the Great becomes Prince of Lithuania (and King of Poland in 1386).
1378	11 August, Battle of the River Voje.
1380	8 September, Battle of Kulikovo Field.
1382	Khan Tokhtamish of the Golden Horde burns Moscow; first recorded use of firearms by Russians.
1385	First Union of the Principality of 'Great Lithuania' (including western Russian principalities) and Kingdom of Poland.
1389–1425	Rule of Vasili I Dmitrievich as Grand Prince.
1395	Army of Timur-i Lenk (Tamerlane) burns town of Elets; confrontation of Russian armies and that of Timur-i Lenk on the River Oka; Timur leaves Russia.
1398–1430	Rule of Prince Vitovt as Prince of 'Great Lithuania' (including western Russian principalities).
1399	Battle of the River Vorskla.
1408	Invasion of Russia by Amir Egidei of the Golden Horde.
1413	Second Union of the Principality of 'Great Lithuania' including western Russian principalities) and Kingdom of Poland.
1425–62	Rule of Vasilii II the Dark as Grand Prince.

ABOVE **The massive medieval earth ramparts of Chernihiv, known as the *Dytynets*, as they appeared at the start of the 20th century. Today these ramparts, along with the 12 cast iron 17th–18th C cannon along their summit, form the M.Kotsyubynsky Central Park of Culture and Recreation. (Chernihiv State Historical Museum photograph)**

BELOW **Russian states, 1466.**
(1) Muscovy, (2) Novgorod, (3) Pskov, (4) Rostov, (5) Ryazan, (6) small principalities, (7) Tver.

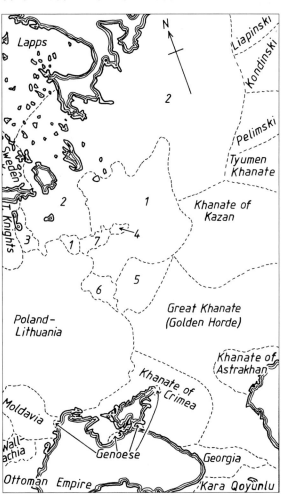

1451	Mongol Prince Mazovsha burns Moscow but fails to take the Kremlin.
1462–1505	Rule of Ivan III Vasilievich as Grand Prince.
1471	Defeat of Novgorod by Moscow at the Battle of River Shelin.
1472	Marriage of Grand Prince Ivan III with Byzantine Princess Sofia Palaeologos.
1478	Novgorod annexed by Moscow.
1480	Death of Khan Ahmad of the Mongol Golden Horde; Russia wins independence from the Golden Horde.
1485	Tver annexed by Moscow.
1485–1516	New Kremlin walls built in Moscow.
1487	First conquest of the Mongol city of Kazan by Moscow (Muscovy).
1493	Grand Prince Ivan III of Moscow proclaims himself Tzar of the whole Rus' (Russian peoples).
1496–97	War between Russia and Sweden; Russia wins an outlet to the Baltic Sea.
1501	Russian invasion of Livonia led by Voivode Shenia, defeating the Teutonic Knights outside Gelmed.

CAMPAIGNS AND BATTLES OF THE 13TH–15TH CENTURIES

This was a very warlike period and, according to the Russian historian M.S.Solovjev, Russia was involved in over 300 conflicts between 1228 and 1462, resulting in 85 full-scale battles. Two hundred of these conflicts involved external enemies – Tatar-Mongols, Lithuanians, Swedes or Teutonic Knights – resulting in 60 battles. If we add at least 150 attacks on fortresses and more than 80 sieges of Russian towns, it becomes clear that there was no prolonged period of peace during these two and a half centuries. Although Russian trade, handicrafts and culture survived, more than 200 years of more or less continual bloody conflict inevitably left their mark on the Russian character.

While vast territories were harassed by the Mongols, Russia's military culture continued to develop rapidly, while there was also considerable external influence. During the mid-13th century, for example, the south-western principality of Galich-Volhynia experienced a notable increase in military power. From c.1240 infantry became more prominent and started to participate in combat on an equal footing with cavalry. The *Ipatjev Chronicles* for 1249, 1251 and 1253 showed that infantry often decided the outcome of such clashes. Furthermore, this southern Russian army now included people from more varied social backgrounds, including townsmen and peasants. Instead of the old term *druzina* (military detachment), troops tended to be called merely 'riders', *peshtsi* or foot soldiers, or simply *vois* – 'warriors' – while the supporting mounted archers were called *streltsi*.

Field battles remained the most important aspect of warfare. As Prince Daniil of Galich reminded his men during their campaign against the Yatvyags in 1251, the 'open field' was their fortress. The fast-moving combats which had characterised Russian warfare against nomadic peoples in the 12th century were no longer common; instead battles were carefully

Details from two miniatures in the *Simonov-Chludov Psalter* dating from around 1270. One, left, illustrates King Nebuchadnezzar with his guards; note that he is apparently depicted wearing mail *chausses*. The other, right, shows King David with two of his soldiers; again, note the pointed helmets, mail aventails, and kite-shaped shields.

planned – though such plans could also change as events unfolded.

Armies still covered up to 80km in one day, or 60km if accompanied by siege equipment. The missile-throwing siege weapons known before the Mongol invasion became even more widespread in the mid-13th century, and the carpenters to build such devices at the site of a siege accompanied an army on the march. This in turn influenced military architecture, with tall stone towers gradually replacing the old wooden ones, initially in the south-west and then in northern Russia.

Prince Daniil of Galich also introduced new elements of Mongol armour and weaponry for his cavalry, including chamfrons and horse-armour like that described by Plano Carpini. Similarly the heavy armour worn by the men improved, the old term *bronja* for armour being replaced by *dospekh*. By the 16th century the latter had come to mean a completely new form of mail-and-plate protection.

The 13th century: resistance to the Crusaders and Mongols

Methods of combat were similarly changing in northern Russia. Thus at the battle of the River Neva a Russian mixed force of cavalry and infantry attacked the Swedes near where the latter had moored their ships, instead of drawing up in a regular battle array as was normal. Meanwhile soldiers of very different social backgrounds now fought side by side.

During the famous 'Battle on the Ice' at Lake Peipus in 1242, the Russians encircled the German 'boar's head' formation of heavily armoured knights – the latter having considerable penetrating power but little manoeuvrability. Similar tactics were repeated in 1268 at the battle of Rakovor (now Rakvere in Estonia), where the Westerners' 'great iron pig' was attacked in its flanks. Here the first of two German 'iron wedges' crushed the forces of Novgorod and Pskov which faced them, but the second wedge then broke from its ambush position to attack the

Two fully armoured warriors in combat, forming a marginal illustration and letter 'M' in a 14th-C Russian manuscript. (*Psalter*, f.291, Saltykov-Shchredrin Public Library, St.Petersburg)

'A king with his guards', as illustrated in the *Chronicle of Georgi Amartola*, Russian, 1318–1327. The soldier on the left, holding a sabre, has a mail aventail across most of his face; the shields are round. (Lenin Library, Moscow)

Russian transport – leaving the first force to be encircled. After four hours' fighting neither side had won a clear advantage, and it was only as evening fell that the greater endurance of the Russians brought them victory. Prince Dovmont of Pskov emerged as the hero of this battle, as recognised even in the German *Rhymed Chronicle*. His unit pursued the retreating Teutonic Knights and eventually reached the Baltic coast before returning with considerable booty.

Soon after the battle of Rakovor, about a thousand German soldiers occupied several frontier settlements in the principality of Pskov. Prince Dovmont immediately took a small number of men in five boats and attacked the enemy on the River Miropovna, the suddenness and speed of the Russian counter-attack enabling Dovmont to defeat a numerically superior foe on St.George's Day, 23 April.

In 1269 the Master of the Teutonic Order, Otto von Rodenstein, gathered all his available troops, numbering almost 18,000, and set off against Pskov in several columns. Some Crusaders went by land, others in river boats bringing large numbers of siege machines with them. Many villages were burned and the well-fortified town of Izborsk was taken by storm. At the end of June the enemy attacked Pskov itself. An initial attack was beaten off, but the subsequent siege lasted ten days, by which time the defenders were almost exhausted. Prince Dovmont led a large crowd of people into the Troitskij Cathedral and, in a solemn ceremony, laid his sword on the altar. There it was consecrated by a procession of priests before Father-Superior Sidor handed the weapon back to Dovmont. This ceremony raised the defenders' morale, and several ferocious sorties were launched against the besiegers; Prince Dovmost himself reportedly even wounding the Teutonic Grand Master. The German Knights then learned that a large relief army was approaching from Novgorod and so, on 8 July, they abandoned their siege. The battles of Rakovor, the Miropovna River and the siege of Pskov brought the long period of aggression from the north-west to an end. They also showed that, despite Mongol massacres, Russia could still defeat the Crusaders.

The battle of Rakovor is also interesting for another reason: before this campaign, catapults called *poroks* were made in the 'Vladika yard' of Novgorod. These were state property, and could apparently be used not only during sieges but also on the battlefield. Catapults were, of course, used during the storming of fortifications. Thus in 1301 the well-fortified Swedish town of Landscrona was, according to the Russian historian Karamzin, taken by

Novgorodians with the help of stone-throwing machines. A contemporary observer also described the Russians approaching Landscrona with abundant light armour and sparkling helmets. 'I suppose', he wrote, 'that they set out on the march in the Russian way,' which probably meant that they moved with their armour displayed to the enemy. This had a tremendous psychological impact.

Meanwhile resistance to the Mongols had started back in 1252 when Prince Andrej Yaroslavich led his troops against the Tatars near Pereyaslavl-Zalesskij; but it was not until 1285 that Prince Dmitrii Alexandrovich drove raiding Tatars from Novgorodian territory, inflicting the first real defeat upon the Mongol occupiers.

The 14th century: development of tactics and army organisation

By comparing the two regions of Russian which escaped complete defeat by the army of Khan Batu, we can see similarities in the structure of Russian armies, in the role of infantry and archers, in tactics, armour, the use of catapults and siege machines as well as a switch to stone fortification. In fact the evidence indicates a speeding up of military development in northern and southern Russia following the Mongol invasion. Clearly a great deal was borrowed from Russia's neighbours, and after 1277 Russian troops also participated in Mongol punitive expeditions to the Caucasus, Lithuania and Poland. From 1269 Russian princes themselves began recruiting troops from the Golden Horde, but this does not necessarily mean that Russian war-craft ceased to be original. On the contrary, the neighbouring Hungarians, Poles and Swedes distinguished 'Russian combat', 'Russian custom' and a 'Russian way' in tactics and armament. Consequently the Russians were able to surprise the Germans by using Tatar weapons; to halt the Tatars with stone-throwing machines and stone-built castles; and to exhaust Baltic Crusaders by Mongol-style archery attacks.

The greatest battle fought by Russians in the 14th century was at **Kulikovo Field (1380)**. Here, fighting alongside traditional cavalry, were large numbers of foot soldiers recruited from the mercantile and peasant classes from all over the country. Craftsmen and petty merchants similarly fought as both infantry and cavalry in Pskov and Novgorod, their role being vital now that an army drawn only from the military élite was no longer adequate. Subsequently farmers and merchants were not accepted into the military, their place being taken by horsemen from the gentry, but in the 14th century the social structure of Russian armies was more mixed.

The size of Russian armies was also increasing, along with the number of formations they contained. At Rakovor in 1268 the Russian army was divided not into the normal three divisions of a large centre

The central panel from a Russian icon illustrating the life and martyrdom of St.George, made in or near Novgorod in the early 14th century. (State Russian Museum, inv.2118, St.Petersburg)

plus two wings, but into four parts. After 1340 the Novgorodians and Muscovites usually went to war in five units. In massed battles such as that of Kulikovo Field there were also, in addition to the large centre and wings, ambush, vanguard and 'watch' formations. In their turn these 'regiments' were subdivided into smaller units comparable to those in a Western European knightly army.

When attacking an enemy, Russian troops usually began the fight with mounted combat, sometimes attacking repeatedly. The evidence also indicates that the highest casualties were usually suffered during this phase. Knightly tradition meant that leaders participated in such combat. However, before the battle of Kulikovo Field in 1380, Grand Prince Dmitrii Ivanovich put on the gear of an ordinary soldier and gave his splendid armour to a *boyar* named Michael Brenk, who took up position beneath the commander's black and white banner, and was subsequently killed. Prince Dmitrii himself fought in the first ranks; he received many blows to the head and body, being severely wounded and twice knocked from his horse, but surviving thanks to his armour.

After the initial cavalry charge a battle tended to become a great mêlée in which men fought hand-to-hand. It is worth noting that independent action by units of horse-archers declined in importance and, from the mid-14th century onwards, was no longer mentioned. Nevertheless Russian cavalrymen continued to use bows, even in the early 16th century, and Muscovite riders impressed foreign visitors by their ability to control reins, bow, arrow, sabre and a horseman's whip.

Battles also traditionally started with duels. The battle of Kulikovo Field began with such a duel between a Tatar warrior named Chelubej and the Russian warrior-monk Peresvet, both being killed by each others' spears on the first pass. The powerful spear blows of Muscovite cavalry crushed the Tatar troops at the battle of the Voja River in 1378. Indeed the Tatar-Mongols themselves began to increase their number of such regiments and to use comparable cavalry tactics of mounted close combat from 1310 onwards. Nevertheless, eye-witness accounts from the late 15th century indicate that the equipment of Mongol warriors of the late Golden Horde was inferior to that of their predecessors in Khan Batu's time.

At Kulikovo Field the superiority of European Russian armament was clear. The poem

ABOVE **Dismounted warrior-saint slaying a dragon from whose belly a previous victim then emerges. Detail from a Russian carved wooden cross made in 1359. (Kremlin Museum, Novgorod)**

Details from an icon of Saints Boris and Gleb, probably painted in Moscow, 14th century. Top, Martyrdom in a boat; above, a prince with his armed following. The shields here are all shown as of 'cropped kite' shape. (Tretyakov Gallery, Moscow)

Zadonshina, written by Sofonij Ryazanets, mentions Lithuanian swords, German *sulits* or short spears, shields from Moscow, helmets of Cherkassk and Tatar origin, and assorted forms of armour. This *Zadonshina* includes more references to European weaponry than did the famous *Epic of Prince Igor* written much earlier. The term *baidana*, which was of Arabic origin and referred to a mail shirt of large flattened rings, was only mentioned once, and it remained one of relatively few Turco-Arabian borrowings in the Russian military vocabulary of the post-Mongol period.

The battle of Kulikovo Field is believed to have lasted four hours and involved numerous controlled and disciplined cavalry combats. By the end of the third hour the Mongols began to waver, yet it was only an attack by the Russian cavalry reserve which clinched the Russian victory – they had been held back by Prince Dmitrii Ivanovich for just such a moment. Surprised by these unexpected reinforcements, the Mongols fled. Nevertheless the cost of the victory was very high: only one-tenth of the Russian army is said to have returned home. Twelve princes and 483 noble *boyars*, the pick of the army, had been killed – representing 60 per cent of the Russian commanders.

Nobody knows the losses among the common soldiers but doubtless the manpower resources of Russia were badly affected by this battle. Medieval sources that claimed that hundreds of thousands of Russian warriors took part are doubtless exaggerated, as were the supposedly huge numbers of Mongols. Clearly 100,000 people preparing for a general battle would represent an uncontrollable horde and such an army certainly could not be arrayed on a battlefield only four or five kilometres wide. Perhaps as many as 36,000 men, forming six divisions, took part but even this was a very large number for the Middle Ages. Even for a major campaign armies were not raised which would exhaust the manpower and other resources of the country. According to the most reliable sources Russian armies of the 15th and 16th centuries could number 100,000 or even 120,000 men, but armies of such a size were intended to operate on several fronts simultaneously rather than all taking part in one battle; the actual size of a *zemstvo* or field army was much smaller.

In 1382 Prince Dmitrii, now nicknamed 'Donskoy' after this great victory (which took place near the Don River), was unable to recruit sufficient troops to face Khan Tokhtamish, whose army then ravaged Moscow. On the other hand, in 1386 Dmitrii Donskoy gathered a considerable force against Novgorod, indicating that Russian manpower had been rebuilt during the intervening four years. For many generations the battle of Kulikovo Field remained a symbol of the struggle for independence, and those who took part were seen as heroes of Russian history. In 1480, the year when Russia finally threw

OPPOSITE **Icon of Saints Boris and Gleb, 14th C, probably from Moscow. (Tretyakov Gallery, Moscow)**

This little drawing was made in the second half of the 14th C, and shares several features with the previous icon painting: a cavalry army is led by a prince or commander wearing the characteristic brimmed hat of the Russian nobility; the horsemen all have the tall, Oriental-style pointed helmets which became almost universal in later medieval Russia; and one carries a 'cropped kite' shield. (*Silvestrovskaya Manuscript*, State Archive of Historical Documents, fund N381, Act.no.53, Moscow)

Icon of St.Demetrius of Thessaloniki, from Pskov, late 14th or early 15th C; the saint carries archery equipment. (Inv.2096, Russian Museum, St.Petersburg)

off the Mongol yoke, Archbishop Vassian urged Ivan III to start a new campaign and encouraged him to repeat the feats of Dmitrii Donskoy.

Nevertheless, the campaigns and battles of the 13th to 15th centuries did reveal shortcomings in Russian military organisation. For example, just three years before the great victory at Kulikovo Field a large Russian force was destroyed by the Tatar Prince Arab-Khan near the **Pjana River (1377)**. On this occasion the Russians failed to send out patrols; left their armour in their wagons; and drank ale and wine as if they were safe at home. Some sources, including the 16th-century *Nikonovskaya Chronicle*, mocked the Russian troops' boasting that one of their number was equal to a hundred Tatars – an over-confidence which would cost them dear when the Tatars secretly encircled the Russian army before attacking its rear.

A combined Russian-Lithuanian-Tatar army suffered a great defeat at the hands of Emir Idegej's troops at the battle of the **Vorskl River (12 August 1399)**, despite the fact that the allied army possessed light bombards, arquebusiers and crossbowmen who were ranged along its front. The battle was long and stubbornly fought, but the end came when some of Idegej's fresh troops attacked at the very moment when the entire Russian-Lithuanian-Tatar army was already committed. The allied leaders, Grand Prince Vitovt and Khan Tokhtamish, fled and almost their entire army was destroyed. According to legend Prince Vitovt lost his way but was led to a place of safety by a Tatar-Kazak named Mamaj. For this service the prince promoted Mamaj to the nobility and granted him land. The Kazak supposedly then founded the Glinskij family; and it was a member of this clan, Elena, who became the mother of Tsar Ivan IV the Terrible.

The flower of Russian-Lithuanian chivalry who had helped Vitovt to establish Great Lithuania and who had also fought under the banners of Dmitrii Donskoj at Kulikovo Field died in this terrible defeat. Idegej then pursued Vitovt as far as Kiev, from which the emir extracted a ransom while his army pillaged southern Russia, causing as much devastation as the original Mongol invasion had done.

The 15th century: Oriental influences, the Mongol decline, and the spread of firearms

Despite such disasters as the Vorskl River, Russia was steadily getting stronger while the Mongol Golden Horde was in decline. Russian military equipment became ever more Oriental in style. Sabres replaced swords, round shields replaced the traditional kite-shape, and various types of Eastern arms and armour were adopted. A battle between Muscovites and Novgorodians in 1455 was the last major combat in which spear-armed cavalry played the leading role; after this the sabre became the primary cavalry weapon. Riding equipment similarly changed with the adoption of lighter, higher Asiatic saddles, whips replacing spurs, and shorter stirrup leathers enabling a rider not only to turn more easily in his saddle but also to use a bow. Some of these features had already been seen in the 12th and 13th centuries but came to dominate in the 14th and 15th. Even in 1500, however, descriptions of combat sound very traditional: 'Clash of spears, crashing of shields, helmets drop down and sabres break, arms are clanging, warriors fall dead and wounded.'

The eastern side, with its entranceway and one gate tower, of the fortress of Koporye, which was constructed in the mid-15th century. (Photograqph V.V.Kostochkina)

In this little sketch of a cavalry battle two horsemen on the victorious side are shown wielding a straight sword and a curved sabre with both hands. One horseman in the retreating army protects himself with what appears to be a so-called 'Lithuanian pavise', with a vertical 'keel' down the front. *Radzilovskaya Chronicle*, in a 15th-C copy of a 13th-C original.

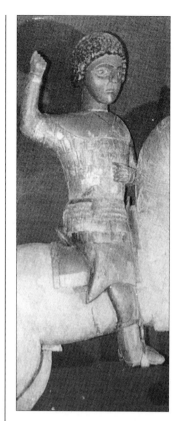

From 1382 firearms start spreading across Russia, firstly as defensive weapons for towns or fortresses, and later as lighter hand-held guns. By the end of the 15th century various types were known, including the *arquebus* which could be carried on a soldier's back, the *samopal* hand-gun, and the *ruchnitsa*, which was a long-barrelled musket. These weapons were not accurate at more than the shortest range, but their fire caused panic among Tatar troops, often making them retreat even before hand-to-hand fighting began. When, in 1480, Khan Ahmed began his ultimately unsuccessful campaign against Russia, the Russians possessed sufficient numbers of cannon and arquebuses to stop his army from crossing the River Ugra. The khan waited on the far bank until autumn, but the Russian defence remained firm and the Tatars eventually retreated. This stand-off resulted in the Mongol-Tatar yoke finally being thrown off after 240 years: Russia became a fully independent state under Tsar Ivan III Vasilievich, who began annexing new territories. Except for his campaigns against the Golden Horde in 1472 and 1480, plus attacks on Kazan in 1467–1469 and 1487, all Ivan III's wars were waged against other Russian states, or again Western neighbours such as Lithuania, Sweden and the Teutonic Knights.

Under Tsar Vasil III the Russian people became acquainted with what they called 'the heavy hand of Moscow'. This became possible because, during the first half of the 15th century, the princes of Moscow found strong support amongst their *dvor* – courtiers or gentry – and the children of the *boyar* aristocracy. This class grew rapidly after the creation of an 'estate system' at the end of the 15th century, as a result of which the interests of the aristocracy and the ruling tsars normally coincided. The aristocracy also provided the tsar with a numerous and efficient army which the ruler used to conquer new lands, distributing these captured territories amongst his soldiers. Although this process was accompanied by economic development, it also relied upon constant territorial expansion.

TOP **Painted wooden statuette of St.George, Russian, 15th century. (Local Historical Museum, Yuriev Polskoy)**

ABOVE **The *kremlin* or citadel of Tver, as illustrated in a detail from a 15th-C Russian icon, showing a variety of types of towers and gates, with characteristic onion-domed Russian churches behind. (Location unknown)**

ARMS AND ARMOUR

Spears and javelins

Russian spears of the 13th to 16th centuries had long triangular heads of diamond section, designed to penetrate armour. During the 13th century *sulitsi* or javelins were also mentioned, eventually being used by both infantry and cavalry to oppose Tatar archery. In fact these darts or javelins were so popular that they became almost universal, not only when approaching the enemy but in hand-to-hand combat and during retreats. Archaeological excavations near Novgorod and Oreshek have uncovered such leaf-shaped dart heads dating from the 13th to 16th centuries. During the 14th century the boar-spear was mentioned as a fighting weapon, having been used for hunting for centuries; however, the largest form of Russian fighting spear did not change, and continued to have a laurel leaf-shaped blade well into the 17th century.

Battle axes

An axe and a boar-spear seem to have been considered the essential arms of a foot soldier in late medieval Russia; one chronicler said of the Muscovites who set out against the Tatars in 1444 that the 'foot-men were equipped with clubs, axes and boar-spears'. In fact two different traditions seem to have merged in the history of the battle-axe. When cavalry dominated warfare this weapon became plebeian, but as armour became stronger and the importance of infantry increased, so the axe rose again in prestige. Amongst the pole-axes, *chekans* and axe-maces with trapezoid blades excavated in Novgorod and Vladimir, some of the former had silver decoration on the blades. These were high quality items made by smiths who exported their products to the neighbouring Saami (Lapps) and Tatars. The popularity of the axe throughout the Mongol period also indicated the strength of the armour worn at this time.

The axe also became a ceremonial parade weapon, and in 1468 a chronicler first mentioned a court functionary called the keeper of the *berdish* or pole-axe. This *berdish* had a crescent moon-shaped blade, and was linked to the long-bladed *berdish* which became common in the later Russian *strelets* army. *Berdishes* were used as a support for hand-held guns, and *streltsi* units equipped with such guns were formed around the last quarter of the 15th century. The long-hafted, broad-bladed *berdish* was designed for swinging blows though it could also be thrust. During the 15th century the *berdish* similarly appeared in Sweden, but as yet the degree of technological interaction between Russia and Scandinavia remains unclear. Meanwhile the cavalry, which was largely recruited from the gentry, made little use of axes.

Swords and sabres

During the 14th century straight swords continued to be used in north-western Russia while sabres were adopted in the south. There is no doubt that the troops of Novgorod and Pskov used straight

The 'boar-spear' or hunting spear of Prince Boris Alexandrovich, Russian, c.1450. The socket is decorated with finely engraved scenes, including a depiction – see detail below – of an archer. (Kremlin Armoury Museum, Moscow)

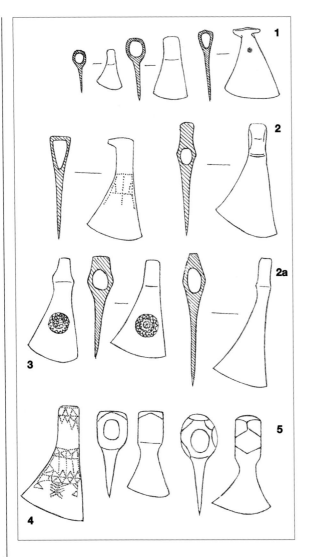

(1) Axes found in the Ipatevski
side-street in Moscow in 1969.
(2, 2a) Axes from Novgorod,
14th–15th C
(3) Axe from Vladimir,
14th–15th C
(4) Axe from Novgorod,
14th–15th C
(5) Axe-maces, 14th–15th C.

cut-and-thrust blades when fighting against Swedes and Germans. At the same time the hilts became longer. Only two Russian swords of this period seem to survive, and one is said to have belonged to Prince Dovmont; it is a thrusting type with a long triangular blade decorated with heavy gilding. Another sword is associated with Prince Vsevolod Mstislavich; this is also decorated with gilded silver, and the motto: 'I will not give my honour to anyone'.

Shortly before the battle of Kulikovo Field another form of straight sword was introduced into Russia. This resembled a plain broadsword and all its parts bore the same names, but it had only one cutting edge. More common were ordinary knightly swords, as seen throughout Eastern Europe. One such weapon with a two-handed hilt and a pear-shaped pommel was found in Pskov; dated to the first half of the 15th century, it indicates that the Russians were using swords of the same type as those used by the Teutonic Knights.

The sabre replaced the sword when fighting against nomad foes from the 15th century onwards, being more convenient for mounted troops. Constant pressure from the Golden Horde encouraged the spread of the sabre and undermined the popularity of the sword, while the zone of transition between one weapon and the other gradually shifted northwards, even reaching Novgorod. Nor was the frontier between the two fashions very clear, with both being used in several regions. It appears that Russian sabre blades were made in essentially the same way as Oriental ones, the finest consisting of folded or layered damascene steel. They could be used for both cutting and thrusting. In the 15th and early 16th centuries they had very pointed blades and straight *krestovina* guards or quillons; one English visitor in the 16th century maintained that Russian sabres were the same as those of the Turks. None seem to survive from the 14th–15th centuries, but examples from neighbouring areas suggest that they were only slightly curved and were therefore more like the sabres of the 13th century than those of the 16th.

Daggers and maces

The *konchar* is first mentioned in the story of the battle of Kulikovo Field in 1380. This substantial fighting knife, whose name came from the Arabic *khanjar*, had a long narrow blade designed to penetrate mail, and was normally carried on the right side of the waist or attached to the saddle. The *konchar* does not seem to have enjoyed great popularity, and there are only a few of them in Russian museums. Otherwise daggers were divided between those carried on the belt, in the boot and under the *saadak* – a name indicating the full array of archery equipment. Belt

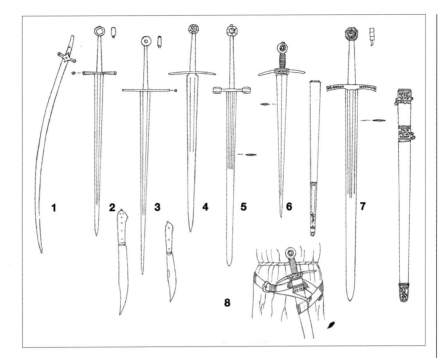

(1) Sabre from the Kuban area, 14th C (State Historical Museum, Moscow)
(2) Sword from Ridomlia, Volhynia region, 14th or early 15th C (State Hermitage Museum, St.Petersburg)
(3) Sword from Vodichki, Khmelnitskaya region, 14th–15th C (Historical Museum, Kamanets-Podolsk)
(4) Sword from Kiev, 14th–15th C (location unknown)
(5) Sword from Sebej, 15th C (State Hermitage Museum, St.Petersburg)
(6) Sword attributed to Prince Dovmont of Pskov, mid-13th C (Historical Museum, Pskov)
(7) Sword attributed to Vselvolod Mstislavich (Historical Museum, Pskov)
(8) Method of scabbard attachment.

knives were short, with two cutting edges and were carried in an *ustie* sheath hung by a hook from the belt. The knife carried beneath the *saadak* was longer and broader, with only one slightly curved cutting edge; it would be attached to the belt on the left side. Boot knives had curved blades. Both *saadak* and boot knives sometimes had a silk or leather braid attached, with a decorative tassel.

Maces and clubs were traditional Russian weapons and some forms were of a surprising originality. For example, square-headed maces with truncated corners appeared in the 12th–13th centuries and continued to be used until the mid-17th. Another crushing weapon, the *shestoper* or 'winged mace', had been used by European knights since the 14th

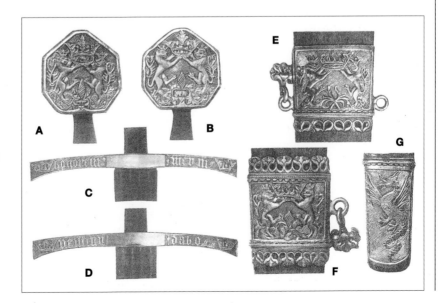

The highly decorated 'sword of Vsevolod Mstislavich' was almost certainly made in central Europe for a Russian prince, perhaps in the late 14th C.
(A & B) The two faces of the pommel
(C & D) The two sides of the quillons
(E & F) The outer faces of the two scabbard mounts
(G) The chape.

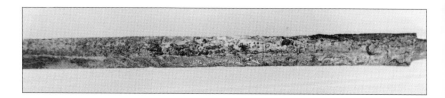

century and was still mentioned in 1502 in Pskov, though by this time the *shestoper* was more a symbol of leadership than a functional weapon.

Crossbows

The many crossbow bolt heads which have been found in Russia shed considerable light on the role of this weapon. The crossbow was clearly important by the 1240s, judging by archaeological evidence from cities destroyed by the invading Mongols. For example, when archaeologists excavated the town of Izyaslavl they found the remains of a crossbowman, apparently a commander, who had perished while defending the gate tower. The spanning belt-hook at his waist is the oldest yet known in Europe. One end of the hook was riveted to the belt while the other formed a doubled hook which would slide over the stock of the crossbow. The device found in Izyaslavl may indicate a transition from the manual method of pulling back the string to a more sophisticated system, perhaps associated with the use of more powerful composite staves. Crossbows spanned by the use of shoulder braces or straps were also recorded in the *Ipatyev Chronicle* in 1291. This system made it possible for a horseman to use a crossbow.

On another occasion the effectiveness of long-range crossbow fire stopped a Mongol army from assaulting the city of Kholm. But, although the power of the crossbow stimulated the development of stronger armour in Western Europe, the effect in Russia is less clearcut, except in the adoption of 'grooved' or 'keeled' pavises by some infantrymen. Nevertheless the crossbow did increase in popularity as never before in Russia, and by the 14th century crossbowmen had become an essential part of any Russian army. As such they continued to fight alongside those who adopted another new weapon – hand-held firearms. It may also be worth noting that the first reference to a cannon being mounted on the walls of Moscow in 1382 described it firing a bolt or arrow rather than a ball – this struck down a Tatar prince. In 1486 the crossbow was mentioned for the last time as a weapon of war, after which it was replaced by muskets, though it continued to be used for hunting.

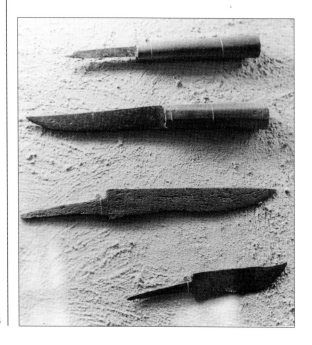

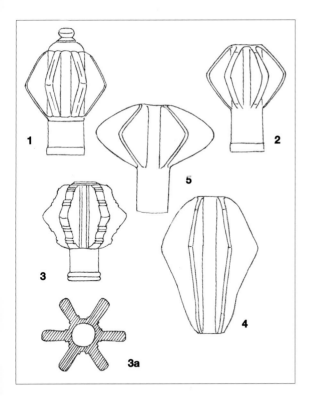

Russian 'winged' maces from Pronsk, Sakhnovka, Khmelnia and Zvenigorod: (1–3, 3a) 13th C; (4–5) 14th C.

Donor figures in the typical costume of wealthy late-medieval Russian men, with a woman on the far right. It was painted in Novgorod in 1467. (Kremlin Museum, Novgorod)

Some crossbow bolt heads were quite massive, being up to four times heavier than ordinary arrowheads. Their 30cm–50cm long shafts reflect their armour-piercing purpose. The heads themselves are usually pyramidal, edged, square or rhomboid in section, and the junction between the head and shaft was clearly designed to cope with a considerable percussive impact. By the 14th and 15th centuries the heads grew even bigger, although the finds from Izyaslavl indicate that crossbowmen were experimenting with heavy bolts even in the first half of the 13th century. Subsequently the heads became thicker with shorter cutting edges, having a somewhat squat appearance. These projectiles were obviously meant to split the plates or scales of armour and cause a broad wound.

Helmets

Judging by manuscript miniatures, icons and written evidence, as well as the contents of the Kremlin Armoury in Moscow, there were two main forms of helmet in use – conical and dome-shaped – both of which had been known in the pre-Mongol period. Prosperous warriors seem to have worn doubled armour and both sorts of helmet, one perhaps forming an 'under-helmet'.

The word *shishak* came from Turkish or Hungarian and could mean an under-helmet. It was mentioned in the will of Grand Prince Ivan Ivanovich in 1359, the first such reference in Europe. The oldest Russian *shishaks* are two examples found by N.S.Shelyapina in 1975 in the well of the Arsenal Tower of Moscow's Kremlin. Their decoration, consisting of a rope-like pattern on the crown and a tendril-like pattern on the top, indicate that they were made in Russia. They are also silvered while the crowns are covered with a copper strip. Having been found alongside an armour and three distinctive spurs, they can be dated around 1500 and may even have been used by late 15th century Muscovite cavalry.

Another typical form of under-helmet had a hemispherical or more rarely a pyramidal crown with additional elements to protect the back of the head, ears and nose, plus a peak. Other evidence from the 16th century indicates that such a *shishak* could be worn beneath a larger helmet.

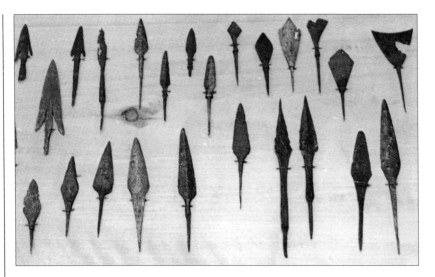

Armour and clothing

During the 13th century Russian military costume underwent considerable changes, and by the mid-century plate armour was being adopted. Unfortunately there is little direct evidence for its detailed appearance during the 14th and 15th centuries. Nevertheless the chronicler of the battle of Kulikovo Field stated that the armour of Prince Dmitrii Ivanovich was severely dented, indicating that it incorporated plates rather than merely being of mail. Such armour was clearly heavy, and for this reason was sometimes abandoned during flight. It could also be destroyed by burning. By the 14th and 15th centuries the plates of such armour might also be exposed, causing it to shine 'like silver', in the words of the chroniclers. See the colour plates and the accompanying illustrations for more particulars.

Bright colours were preferred for military clothing, with miniature paintings indicating that blue, green or red were popular. Capes and cloaks are usually depicted as green; shields as red or red and green, sometimes with a herringbone pattern of green, white, brown, red and black. Sword scabbards are shown as red or brown, banners usually red. Red was synonymous with 'beautiful' in the Russian language – hence such phrases as 'red girl' or 'the red sun' – and perhaps this was why red-coloured shields seem to have been the most popular.

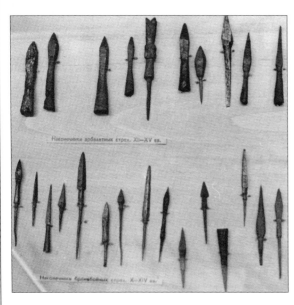

Russian arrowheads, and crossbow bolt heads, found in Novgorod. (Kremlin Museum, Novgorod)

FORTRESSES AND SIEGE WARFARE

In the 1240s multistorey stone towers were built in south-western Russia, some as tall as 30m (100ft) high, to guard the approaches to gates. Such towers were also designed so that their defenders could continue shooting at the enemy even if they broke into the rest of the fortress. In fact their primary function was as bases for long-range shooting. Comparable towers were erected in western Russia in the second half of the 13th century; 15 have been recorded, though the original number is likely to have been greater in the principality of Volhynia alone. Similar constructions were even erected in villages and temporarily conquered towns, presumably to prevent Mongol raiding. They seem to have proved so effective as 'bases of fire' that they began to appear in northern Russia in the mid-14th century. Citadels made entirely of stone came later, though Daniil Romanovich had a new stone-built capital at Kholm as early as 1259.

Russian wars of the 13th to 16th century increasingly focused on the conquest and annexation of territory; consequently, fortified centres similarly increased in importance. A third of the 460 recorded campaigns between 1228 and 1462 involved attacks upon, and the defence of, towns. During the period of the 'Mongol Yoke' various ways of protecting territory evolved, depending on local circumstances; these similarly effected the function of fortifications. Following the Mongol invasion under Khan Batu, Tatar raiders avoided using cumbersome heavy transport and siege equipment, and seldom risked assaulting towns. If they were few in number they contented themselves with ravaging the rural outskirts, but if they were sufficiently numerous they might try to take a fortress by deception or by defeating its garrison in open battle.

Conditions were different on the north-western and western frontiers, where the Teutonic Knights and Lithuanians often relied on siege engines to take towns. Hence there was a large-scale programme of fortification and of assembling numerous stone-throwing machines from the late 13th century onwards. After fortifying their capital cities in 1302–09 the people of Pskov and Novgorod erected many fortresses, especially along their borders. As wooden and earthen defences became obsolete, many were replaced by stronger stone structures. New fortified towns were created in strategically vulnerable regions, including Koporye, Korela, Oresheck, Izborsk, Yama and Porkhov.

Between 1382 and 1426 firearms began to be used in attack as well as in defence of Russian fortifications, alongside existing siege weapons. The walls and towers were themselves designed to allow their defenders to employ arquebus fire, archery and crossbows, but it was not until the second quarter of the 15th century that firearms really changed the design of military architecture. The earliest evidence within Russia appears to be the thickening of the walls of Porkhov in 1430, followed by the rebuilding of Yamgorod in 1448.

During the second half of the 15th century, coinciding with the formation of the Muscovite state, cannon became powerful enough to breach stone walls. The first case in Russian history was in 1481, during the siege of the Teutonic Knights' fortress at Fellina. Another new stage was reached with the construction of the strictly quadrangular citadel of Ivangorod in 1492, the first such structure in Russia. But as Russian architects were generally imitating Western European fortifications, even Ivangorod seemed old fashioned for its date, and lacked flanking towers. This weakness became very apparent when a Swedish force easily captured the new fortress only four years after it had been built. Ivangorod was thereafter modernised and strengthened to cope with siege warfare based entirely upon cannon.

The following years saw remarkably rapid improvements in Russian military architecture, especially in the south, and resulted in Russia becoming one of the most advanced countries in Europe in this field of warfare. Nor is it a coincidence that these changes took place as Russia became a unified state. They also reflected the fact that wars were now largely resolved through sieges whereas in earlier times they had been decided in open battle.

The fortified tower at Stolpye, built during the second half of the 13th or first half of the 14th century. Apart from a few largely symbolic stone gates in major cities, this type of isolated tower was the first form of stone fortification to be constructed in Russia. They appeared in the westernmost principalities, probably as a result of Central European influence, and would not be seen further east for many years.

The free-standing round tower at Kamenets was built in the second half of the 13th century. Known as the 'White Tower', it was probably inspired by comparable frontier defences in Hungary or Poland. (Photograph G.N.Logvina)

Timber fortifications

A distinctive Russian style of fortress began to appear in the 13th and 14th centuries, achieving its highest development in the 16th and 17th centuries. The shape of a Russian town was, of course, determined by its walls, towers, religious buildings and the basic contours of the landscape. Up to the 13th century any inhabited site with any form of barrier defence was called a 'town', but other more specific terms gradually emerged. These including *tyn*, meaning a paling or stockade, and *gorodni*, *tarasy* and *ostrog* to designate certain types of wall construction.

A *tyn* or paling was the simplest and oldest type of wooden fortress wall. It consisted of moats and ramparts which could reach a considerable height. Logs were used to support the paling walls, the sharpened ends of these logs often protruding outside the wall – these were called 'needles'. *Polaty* were scaffolds constructed along the inner side of such timber walls to support them. Walls in which palings were combined with such a framed construction were, of course, much more stable.

In the slanting *ostrog* the sharpened logs were inclined inwards, presenting a smooth, hard-to-climb glacis, while the wall itself was supported by a low earth embankment, plus a special interior *kozly* or scaffold erected close to the wall. The most obvious advantage of these timber defences was the rapidity and simplicity of their construction. The greatest disadvantage was that the lower end of the logs which formed the wall soon began to rot.

Those with a framed construction were called *gorod*, *gorodni* or *tarasy*, referring to a much stronger and more complex form of architecture. Their walls were normally twice as high as the simple *tyn* or paling, and were generally as thick as a *tyn* was high. In fact the *gorod*, *gorodni* or *tarasy* seem to have been developed in response to the appearance of firearms, especially cannon. Each was slightly different. The *tarasy* consisted of two parallel walls with a substantial distance between them, these walls being connected by cross-pieces at regular intervals. Some of the bays so formed were filled with rubble, but other, often broader bays remained empty and were used as defensive positions for members of the garrison. Each of these bays normally had two loopholes and a door.

Gorodni were separate frames built close to one another. One weakness of such a wall was that the junction of the frames began to rot very quickly, and the walls consequently became crooked. Furthermore their construction required a great deal of time as well as building materials. Loopholes were similarly added to such walls.

Up to the 13th century there were no towers inside these sorts of fortress, their eventual appearance again resulting from the introduction of gunpowder artillery. Later medieval Russian fortresses had many types of tower depending on their function and construction. The most common terms for these were *veja*, *strelnitsa*, *koster* and *stolp*, while the term 'tower' only came into use in the 16th century. These categories included the corner tower plus gate, the round tower, the four-angled tower, the two-tiered tower, the closed tower in the centre of a wall, and various others. Such wooden towers differed in their shapes, purpose, number of storeys, and the wood from which they were constructed.

The number of towers and their dimensions naturally reflected the fortress's size and importance. If the shape of the latter followed the contours of the land, round towers were usually used. If the shape of the fortress was more geometrical, then four-sided towers tended to be constructed, because they were not only easier to connect to the walls in a regular manner, but also provided a wider field of fire.

Towers were also used for such purposes as storage barns, accommodation, churches and chapels. It was, in fact, normal for larger fortresses to have a balcony-like chapel suspended over the entrance gates; this not only helped defend the gate itself but also served as a religious focus which offered the protection of the saints to the most vulnerable point in the fortification. The largest towers incorporated sentry boxes which had windows on all sides, as well as railed galleries providing a commanding view over the surrounding countryside.

Fortress details are usually divided into two groups. The first includes defensive systems directly forming part of the main defensive structure, such as *oblams* (see below), loopholes and so on. The second includes additional devices such as ditches, embankments, etc. which were usually constructed around towns and prisons.

The *oblam* was a second form of frame construction above the lower part of the wall or tower, although sometimes the upper part of the frame wall itself could be called an *oblam*. In towers it was normally built over the entire upper surface, whereas walls only had *oblams* on their outside surface. Loopholes took the form of small windows through which the defenders could shoot, their dimensions depending on their choice of weapon. They were, however, usually about 8cm–10cm (3ins–4ins) wide. On the outside the lower and lateral edges were sloped to provide a better angle for shooting. When larger guns were introduced the dimensions of such embrasures naturally increased, sometimes up to 30cm–40cm (12ins–16ins) wide.

During the 8th to 10th centuries deep moats with steep sides had commonly been a vital feature of the defences, but from the 10th century onwards the ramparts themselves became more important, eventually reaching 10m–16m (roughly 30ft–50ft) in height.

At the end of the 15th century the whole northern territory reaching as far as the Arctic coast was

Reconstruction of the Kremlin or citadel of Moscow as it probably appeared in the mid-14th C, when the fortifications were still made entirely of timber; the only stone structures in this scene are the churches on the skyline.

Tower Three of the Kremlin in Novgorod, seen from Tower Four. Tower Three is 15th C, and the broken wall between the towers can be seen to consist of two brick facings filled with a rubble core. (D.Nicolle photograph)

incorporated into the Russian state. Devastating raids by the neighbouring people of Pomoriya resulted in the construction of fortresses even in this remote region. In addition to large fortresses, many monasteries, small *ostrogs* and *pogosts* or administrative outposts were erected, all of them combining to form a powerful system of defence in depth to stop invasions along the northern rivers.

The *ostrog* at Kola was first mentioned as early as the 13th century, and since it formed the vital northernmost outpost of Russia its fortifications were rebuilt several times. Even so, the walls of such fortresses continued to be made of timber until the 18th century, normally using a timber framework construction where *gorodni* alternated with *tarases*. Empty bays were again left in the walls of such fortifications, being used to store food and other supplies, just as would be the case in the better known Siberian fortresses. Meanwhile most towers in this northern region were built in the form of irregular hexagons with doubled outer walls.

Ustyug was the next most important of these fortified northern outposts. It had first appeared as early as the mid-12th century, and by the 17th century it consisted of two parts known as Gorodishche and Great Ostrog. These had 24 towers and timber paling walls with interior defensive galleries; meanwhile a wide moat, 3.5m (11.5ft) deep, protected Ustyug from the north-east.

Another distinctive feature of defensive architecture in the north of Russian was that many fortresses with stone inner walls also had timber outer walls. One such fortress-city was Novgorod itself. Prefabrication was used to speed up the building of some fortresses and there were markets selling the prefabricated elements for buildings in most Russian towns. Polotsk is an example of a town that was built by using such prefabrication techniques.

The southern fortresses of Russia were in the most vulnerable area, and here entire lines of fortifications had been built (see MAA 333: *Armies of Medieval Russia 750–1250*). Meanwhile the development of Siberia on the eastern frontier of Russia began in the 14th and 15th centuries. Here the first small *ostrogs* were built to defend newly acquired territory from enemy raids or invasion. These, as well as the comparable *slobodas* or fortified winter encampments, steadily increased in number. Thereafter they continued to serve as military and administrative centres

CAVALRY, 1250–1300
1: Western Russian cavalryman, fully armoured
2: Boyar nobleman from Pskov
3: South-Eastern Russian cavalryman

INFANTRY, 1250–1325
1: Russian crossbowman
2: Urban militiaman
3: Light infantry archer

B

CAVALRY, 1300–75
1: Western Russian light
   cavalryman, c.1350
2: Western Russian heavy
   cavalryman, c.1375
3: Novgorod urban
   cavalryman, c.1350

C

INFANTRY, 1325–1400
1: Dismounted nobleman, mid-14th century
2: Infantryman, Suzdal, mid-14th century
3: Crossbowman, late 14th century

D

EASTERN RUSSIA, 1375–1425
1: Cavalryman, late 14th century
2: Mounted drummer, early 15th century
3: Prince in gilded armour, late 14th century

E

WESTERN RUSSIA & 'GREAT LITHUANIA', 15TH C

1: Heavy cavalryman, early 15th century
2: Novgorod noble cavalryman, mid-15th century
3: Infantryman, late 15th century

F

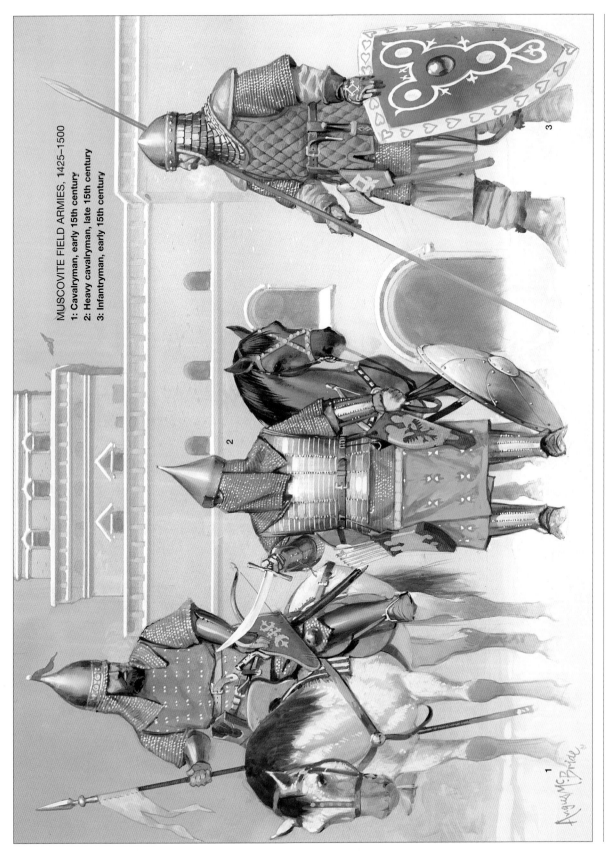

MUSCOVITE FIELD ARMIES, 1425–1500
1: Cavalryman, early 15th century
2: Heavy cavalryman, late 15th century
3: Infantryman, early 15th century

MUSCOVITE GARRISONS, c.1450–1500
1: Dismounted horse-archer, end of 15th C
2: Musketeer, mid-15th C
3: Dismounted officer, end of 15th C

Tower Two of the Novgorod Kremlin. This particularly massive part of the brick fortifications was built in the 14th–15th C and is one of the earliest towers. (D.Nicolle photograph)

as well as centres of trade well into the 18th century. The most widely used type of fortress in Siberia was the *ostrog*, the simplest of these consisting of winter encampments surrounded by paling walls. Subsequently wooden towers were added to many of them.

Siege machinery

The earliest Russian attempts to use siege engines may have been during the Russo-Byzantine War of AD 968–971, but thereafter they are not mentioned in the chronicles for several centuries. In 1237–1240, however, the Mongols used machines of Chinese or Central Asian form – known as *porocki* – to take more than ten large Russian cities. Without a doubt the Mongol conquerors were primarily responsible for a large-scale adoption of this stone-throwing weapon which, during the second half of the 13th century, became an indispensable means of both assaulting and defending town walls. For example, in south-western Russia they are mentioned in 1245 and 1260, and in the north in 1268 and 1301. In the 14th century stone-throwing engines were used by armies and were kept in the military stores of larger Russian towns; Moscow had such machines in 1382. The early 14th to early 15th centuries witnessed the high point in the development of the stone-throwing *porocki,* which continued to be used for many years alongside cannon. During the first decades of the 15th century, however, their use declined, and by 1450 *porocki* were abandoned altogether.

The growing power of beam-sling devices was made possible simply by increasing their size and making a stronger beam out of several springy poles lashed together. By taking the most reliable data into account, we can estimate that a Russian stone-throwing machine could be up to 8m (26ft) high, might weigh 5 tons, and could hurl stones weighing 60kg (130lbs) and more. From 50 to 250 men seem to have been required to operate the largest machines.

A disadvantage was that such machines did not have a long effective life, and to ensure that they were available for serious operations the inventory had to be constantly renewed. Special experts called *popochnye* supervised their production; to construct a stone-throwing machine a man had to have sufficient knowledge of mathematics to make the necessary precise technical calculations. Furthermore he needed to know the special artillery commands, to say nothing of maintaining his machines' efficiency. These devices were built, repaired and stored in many regional capitals, which presupposes quite a large number of technically qualified personnel.

Different types of stone-throwing machinery were, of course, used in Russia, and as the years passed more effective or accurate beam-sling machines were introduced. They included those with a moveable counterbalance, which became very popular. Nevertheless, despite their increasing power and accuracy, stone-throwing machines eventually proved unable to deal with stone fortifications, and were superceded by far more effective gunpowder weapons.

FIREARMS

Firearms first appeared in Russia between 1376 – when an unidentified device opened up against Russian troops from behind the walls of a Volga Bulgar city – and 1382, when cannons and *tyufyaki* (handguns) took their place alongside crossbows and stone-throwing *porocki* to defend the walls of Moscow. It seems logical to assume that this new weapon was brought to Moscow during the period of active military preparations which preceded the battle of Kulikovo Field.

Written records offer the following dates for the storage and use of guns in Eastern Europe and Asia: 1374 by the Teutonic Knights; 1378–1381 in Hungary; 1382 in Lithuania; 1383 in Poland and Bohemia; the 1360s and 1370s in Mamluk Egypt; 1389 in Turkey; 1379 in Central Asia; 1399 in India; and 1366 in China. In all these examples the records consider the event noteworthy, though the first experiments might have been carried out a little earlier; furthermore, the first instance of the use of such guns nearly coincided with the first wave of the weapons' spread across Central, Northern, and Eastern Europe – these dates are all remarkably close to one another.

The words used to denote the first Muscovite guns suggest that such artillery came from two different sources; from the Germans, Poles and Lithuanians in the west, and from the Black Sea or Middle East to the south; generally speaking, however, a Western source seems most likely.

By around 1400 there were undoubtedly arsenals containing guns in major Russian capital cities like Novgorod, Pskov, Tver and Moscow, while the guns themselves were probably produced by local locksmiths. Matters begin to change in the middle of the 15th century, around the time when cities began to fall with the help of firearms. Soon cannon proved themselves capable of breaching fortifying walls. Even in the open these new guns were showing how effective they could be, and in 1480, during the confrontation on the Ugra River, Muscovite marksmen hit a good many Tatars 'with arrows and arquebuses, and drove them off the river bank'. This episode deserves notice as the first recorded case of the use of firearms in open combat in Russia.

The massive Russian fortress of Ivangorod overlooks the River Narva in the Baltic coastal region. Built between 1496 and 1507, it directly faces the rival castle of Hermannsburg on the other bank of the river – the most easterly fortress of the Teutonic Knights in Estonia, while Ivangorod marked the Russian frontier.

Beginning with the 1471 campaigns against Novgorod, Tver, Fellin, Serpeysk and Vyborg, Muscovite gunners also began to play a decisive offensive role. Aristotle Fioroventy, who came to Moscow in 1475, then established one of the few large gun foundries in Russia. Thereafter in 1484, 1490, 1494, 1504, 1507 and 1513 Greek, Italian, German, Scottish and other gun-making experts came to Russia, confirming the enthusiasm and intensity with which these weapons were adopted. One musket barrel, two original cannon and 28 descriptions of similar items have survived from this period. By comparing groups of these weapons we may conclude that a standardised casting system existed. The moulds, and thus the resulting barrels, were of uniform calibre and length, apparently being created by the use of identical measuring devices. In fact later castings were identical in their technical specifications, except that the barrels became heavier. This standardisation must have made possible the large-scale casting of gun barrels, and as a result it did not take long for the entire firearms arsenal of Russia to be re-equipped and modernised. Thus, long before Peter the Great's military reforms at the start of the 18th century, official regulations put an end to unauthorised gun production. The generally accepted idea that there was minimal uniformity and general disorder in Old Russian military production before Peter the Great is clearly untrue.

Descriptions of the weapons cast by experts named Yak in 1483 and Pyotr in 1501 make it clear that gun carriages also existed. The introduction of gun carriages permitted the development of field artillery, just as happened in the Hussite armies of Bohemia. An Italian named Pavel Jovy wrote, according to his interpreter Dmitri Gerasimov, that: 'In the Moscow Kremlin can be seen many copper (probably meaning bronze) cannons cast by the skill of Italian masters and placed upon wheels'. This context would seem to suggest that Pavel Jovy was referring to guns whose wheeled carriages greatly increased their mobility and enabled them to be used in the field, just as they were in the battle of the Ugra River in 1480.

In addition to the manufacture of guns in Moscow, facilities to produce cast

A reconstruction of the fortified wooden 'town' of Olgov overlooking the River Oka, as it would have appeared in the 13th century. (G.V.Boriseivich)

Sections through reconstructions of the various configurations of *tyn* or timber paling wall as used from the 13th to 16th C, from the simplest stockade, through the more elaborate *ostrog* sloping types, to the incorporation of scaffolding-framed inner works. (O.V.Tymkina)

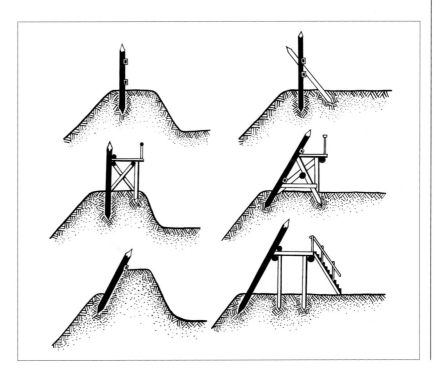

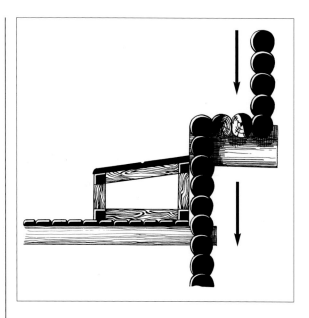

Section through the upper part of a timber wall fortification with an overhanging gallery. Note the hole cut through the upper floor, to enable defenders to shoot downwards or to drop missiles on attackers. (O.V.Tymkina)

Reconstruction of a stretch of *tarasy* type timber fortification, showing two bays filled with rubble or earth for added strength, and two left empty for occupation by defenders. (O.V.Tymkina)

iron cannonballs and to manufacture gunpowder were established, these first being mentioned in 1494; this evidence indicates a transition to granulated powder production instead of the previous and less practical 'powder pulp'. In 1513, according to one witness, up to 2,000 large and small arquebuses were used during the assault on Smolensk. Paralleling this rapid increase in the number of guns available came a notable improvement in their quality.

Cannon are usually the first firearms to be given descriptive names, and in the oldest records they are sometimes called 'great'. From 1382 onwards cannon are consistently mentioned in the defence of towns. From 1399 onwards they were used in *wagon-burg* field fortifications as well as during assaults on various forms of fortification. Some sources emphasize the gigantic size of so-called 'great cannons'; we have mention of cannon being drawn on 40 carts in 1463, and on other occasions of them bursting after their first test firing, or making no more than three shots before failing. Nevertheless, despite their great weight and technical imperfections these massive weapons did breach town walls, and caused such damage that a city might surrender after the first bombardment.

The making of a 1,000-ton 'great' cannon in 1448 was marked out as an event of state importance. Though constructed much later, in 1585, the famous 'Tsar Cannon' made by Andrey Chokhov was based upon mid-15th-century designs, although it was two and a half times heavier than any of its Russian predecessors. This gun, with a calibre of 92cm and a length of 534cm (36.2ins x 209.5ins) may well have been the biggest in the world.

The balls used for 'wall breaking' in 15th-century Russian cannon were often described as being 'knee-' or 'waist-high'. They were, of course, still made of stone. Then, at the end of the 15th century, a new form of high trajectory gun appeared in Russia, a mortar designed to breach the 'vaults' within a fortress. On the other side of the wall, such monster guns were not manoeuverable enough to be practical in the defence of towns. Instead small wall-mounted cannon were frequently mentioned up to 1471, and they proved quite adequate for the task.

In addition to cannons, the chronicles mentioned *tyufyaki*. They were normally used in defence of fortified centres, as in 1382, or while

attacking such fortifications, as in 1408. Towards the end of the 15th century *tyufyaki* were no longer used by field troops, but were still used in defence of fortifications. The word *tyufyak* (Russian plural *tyufyaki*) comes from the common Turco-Persian-Arab term *tufak* or *tyufenk,* which originally meant a blow-pipe used as a hunting weapon. It may then have been used to project 'Greek fire', but soon came to mean the earliest form of light or hand-held gun. The word survived in the Middle East and eventually referred to a rifle. For their part the Russians even used the name *tyufyak* for guns that were specifically stated to be of German origin, so the use of an Oriental term did not necessarily imply an Oriental design for the gun in question. It does, however, seem possible that the word *tyufyak* did indicate a gun with a broad or even slightly funnel-shaped muzzle.

Tyufyaki of the 15th century were not only used defensively but also when raiding towns; but to shoot a light gun at fortified walls hardly makes sense, so perhaps some other device was involved. In fact a book called *The Cannons and Arquebuses Description Book* unexpectedly mentions *tyufyaki* with calibres of from 4cm up to 8.5cm (1.57ins to 3.3ins). Perhaps *tyufyaki* were originally intended as anti-personnel weapons, with relatively short 'blunderbuss' barrels firing multiple projectiles. During the course of development of the earliest firearms this design may have been generally replaced by more accurate small-bore single-shot weapons in the last quarter of the 15th century, resulting in the *tyufyak's* disappearance.

Arquebuses are mentioned by the chronicles during attacks on cities from 1408 onwards, and in defence of cities from 1450; then in the 1470s this weapon increased in importance, leaving the *tyufyak* far behind. Such a development may have reflected the increasing efficacy and reliability of metallic bullets. The earliest arquebuses whose design can be described in more or less exact detail appeared during the final quarter of the 15th century. All were made in the Moscow gun foundry and bore the inscription 'arquebus', together with the maker's name and a date. They also had the extended barrels typical of the true arquebus. The earliest surviving bronze example has a wooden traversing handspike instead of the normal butt-stock and, judging by comparable Swedish and German examples, dates from between 1400 and 1450.

A Russian hand-gun, 1375–1450. The short barrel is firmly fastened to a long wooden stock by two metallic bands. (State Historical Museum, Moscow)

Reconstruction of a stretch of *gorod* type timber fortification with one timber tower. (O.V.Tymkina)

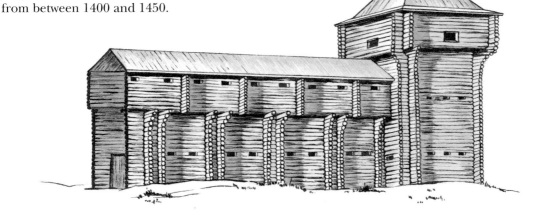

CONCLUSIONS

The abundant military arsenal created in Russia by the 1240s demonstrates that the country was technologically advanced. This continued to be true of later decades and, despite the Mongol occupation, developments sometimes advanced at an even greater pace. The arms and armour used from the 14th to 16th centuries were in many ways based on the experience of the 13th century. At a time when the very existence of the Russian nation was threatened, the cost and importance of armour and weaponry doubtless increased. At the same time Russian craftsmen actively looked at home and abroad for military innovations, adopting those which were suitable and developing them to the needs of their own fighting men. This process was particularly intensive during the reigns of Daniil of Galich, Dmitrii Donskoy and Ivan III. As a result Russian military equipment and training were at the same levels as those of Russia's eastern and western neighbours. Indeed Russian soldiers often astonished the former and impressed the latter with their skill, bravery and equipment.

Russian troops were clearly armed with modern types of weapon. Archaic arms and armour were excluded and those that were used were characteristic of a prosperous and progressive country on a par with the rest of Europe. In fact several typical pieces of Russian gear were more advanced than those seen to the west; for example tall spiked helmets, brigandine-type body armours, *berdishi* long-hafted infantry axes, specialised pavise shields or mantlets, notably large crossbow bolts, and short-barrelled hand-held arquebus firearms. Even during the period when Russia was suffering its worst blows in both the north and south of the country, during the second half of the 13th century, there were continuing improvements in military skills and associated technology, particularly where infantry were concerned. This was paralleled by improvements to stone-throwing machines, stone fortifications and eventually firearms.

Such technological progress was closely connected with an elaboration of military tactics, especially concerning hand-to-hand combat in open formations during the second half of the 14th century. Armies were established to defend the entire country, north and south, together with a system of stone fortresses, most notably in the north-west of the country and along its southern frontier. Throughout the Middle Ages open field battles remained the central feature of campaigns and generally defined their outcome. Yet the forms changed, towards a prolonged and tactically

The Vyshka and Ryabinovka Towers of the fortress at Old Izborsk, erected in the late 14th century. (Photograph A.A.Alexandrova)

more complicated kind of combat involving more mobile units. This was similarly accompanied by the establishment of a numerous and disciplined officer corps, a professional military élite, and the enlistment of bond-farmers who owed military obligations to the state. The army was strengthened by engineer and artillery corps, as well as with crossbowmen. In general soldiers became more flexible and varied in their military capabilities. By the time the 'Mongol Yoke' was finally shaken off a unified Russian state had been established. The Mongol invasion did not separate Russia from the rest of European technological culture, and it could be fairly said that the battle of Kulikovo Field (1380) was largely won with European weaponry.

Miniature from a 15th-C copy of the lost 13th-C *Radzilovskaya Chronicle*, showing a mounted force attacking the gate of a town or castle.

Amongst the countries which bordered the Baltic Sea, Russia was far ahead in the production and use of new kinds of shields, especially pavises; plate armour, rowel spurs and tall, pointed helmets. In fact there is evidence that Russian brigandine armours, helmets, leather pauldrons or shoulder protectors and perhaps shields may have been exported to Scandinavia, Poland, Hungary and the German Military Order of Teutonic Knights. This would have encouraged a certain degree of uniformity in the military equipment seen around the Baltic. A comparable tendency might also be found in siege catapults, crossbows and cannon, as well as in the design and construction of towered fortresses.

Despite a general trend towards unification, the necessity for the Russians to fight on two fronts, just as they had in the 11th and 12th centuries, resulted in the establishment of a corps of heavily armoured cavalry in Novgorod-Pskov, the weaponry of such horsemen being notably heavier than the arms and armour seen in southern Russia. In fact this tactical and technological division effectively established two geographical zones characterised by the use of plate and mail armour, swords and sabres, infantry pavises and round cavalry shields, crossbows and hand bows, spurs and lashes, stone forts and a system of defence based upon field patrols. On the other hand there was never an absolute division between those weapons designed to fight European foes and those intended for use against Turco-Mongol threats. Infantry from the northern towns took part in the battle of Kulikovo Field near the Don, and cavalrymen from Moscow campaigned far to the north. Heavy pavises which were rested upon the ground, rowel spurs, crossbows, cannons and arquebuses were used in the struggle against the Tatars, while sabres and bows were used against Teutonic Knights along the Livonian frontier. Formidable *kremlins* or citadels were just as much a feature of Moscow and Suzdal as they were of Novgorod and the north.

In his treatise entitled *Politics*, which was written between 1663 and 1666, Y. Krizhanich commented on this feature of Russian military

Detail from the left-hand side of the *Icon of the Miracle of the Virgin Mary of the Sign*, painted in the 1460s. It shows two noblemen – note their hats – riding out of Novgorod, which is defended by troops assembled beneath the icon of the Virgin Mary, which supposedly saved the city from Suzdalian conquest. The armoured defenders carry spears and kite-shaped shields. (Museum of the History of Art and Architecture, Novgorod)

affairs: 'Russian methods of warfare belong to an intermediate level between those of the Scythians (meaning the Turks and Tatars) and those of the Europeans. Scythians only use light weapons while the Europeans almost exclusively use heavy ones. We, in our turn, use both kinds quite effectively. We may imitate the tactics of both peoples, though we cannot outdo them. Compared to the Scythians we are much stronger when using our heavy arms and almost as skilful as they are when in using light arms. It is completely the opposite with the Europeans. That is why we should use weapons of both kinds against our enemies and should take advantage of this situation.'

These words, written by a commentator who was a near-contemporary of the events, sum up the very essence and distinctiveness of medieval Russian warfare. In fact it was only after the end of the 15th century that Russian cavalry adopted a much larger degree of Oriental equipment, especially in terms of sabres and padded saddles. This increase in Oriental military influence was associated with the start of the long Russian struggle against the Khanate of the Crimea, and also with the recruitment of large numbers of Tatars into the Muscovite army.

Russian military history during the later medieval period can therefore be divided into the following phases:

1240–1350 This was a period of healing the wounds caused by the Mongol conquest and recouping the country's strength. The territory of the Russian states was drastically reduced, but in the north and south-west resistance to the Mongol and other intruders was organised. In terms of tactics and armament, what had been called 'the Russian way' was preserved and indeed its effectiveness was considerably increased.

1350–1400 These years were characterised by an astonishing growth of military technology and a switch from defensive to offensive operations. This period also largely coincided with the activities of Prince Dmitrii Ivanovich Donskoy (1359–1389), and the appearance of the first stone fortifications in Moscow (1367). In addition to the struggle against the Mongol-Tatar Golden Horde, the Russian states had to resist Lithuanian expansion. Meanwhile the concepts of centralised military leadership and of greater military discipline grew stronger, and pan-Russia mobilisations became common. Moscow created a large army recruited from across Russia, mainly using European weapons and tactics; and eventually this army defeated the Tatars at the great battle of Kulikovo Field, one of the most significant clashes of the Middle Ages. The Mongols were not yet totally defeated, but the myth of their invincibility had been shattered. In Moscow and other cities firearms were eagerly adopted as soon as they became available. Russian troops continued to use traditional tactics of preventive field patrols along the Oka River frontier against the Golden Horde. The need to erect stone fortifications became obvious, while at the same time the methods of siege warfare used by the Mongol-Tatars steadily fell behind those of the Russian armies.

1400–1480 These were the years during which Russia gathered its strength for a decisive strike which ended in the country shaking off the 'Mongol Yoke'. This victorious 'springtime' in Russian history also coincided with a fundamental break in the traditional system of armament and tactics. Sabre-armed cavalry replaced spearmen, while artillery and *streltsi* armed with guns emerged as new military formations.

To summarise, we may say that the 13th to 15th centuries were a period during which the achievements of pre-Mongol Russia were not only preserved but reinforced, at the time when the very existence of Russia itself was threatened. In conditions of truly titanic struggle on several fronts, and in the face of feudal division, a solid Russian state was established, with Moscow as its capital.

FURTHER READING

Allsen, T.T., 'Mongol Census-Taking in Rus', 1245–1275', *Harvard Ukrainian Studies* V/1 (March 1981) 32–53

Belovinski, L.V., *S Russkim Voinon Cherez Veka (With the Russian Warrior across the Centuries)*, in Russian (Moscow 1992)

Billington, J., *The Icon and the Axe: An Interpretive History of Russian Culture*, (New York 1966)

Borisov, N.C., *Russkie Polkovodsi XIII–XVI vv. ('Russian Military Leaders of the XIII–XVI Centuries')*, in Russian (Moscow 1993)

Cherniavsky, M., 'Khan or Basileus: An Aspect of Russian Medieval Political Theory', *Journal of the History of Ideas*, XX (1959) 459–476

Crummey, R.O., *The Formation of Muscovy 1304–1613* (London 1987)

The army of Novgorod, aided by an angel, defeats the invading army of Suzdal, in the *Icon of the Miracle of the Virgin Mary of the Sign*, 1460s. In the foreground are spear-armed heavy cavalry; note also at upper centre two clearly painted curved sabres. (Museum of the History of Art and Architecture, Novgorod)

Dzis, I., & A.Sherbakov, 'Novgododtsi Vremen Kulikovskoy Bitvi 1380' ('Novgorod Warriors of the time of the Battle of Kulikovo, 1380'), in Russian, *Zeughaus* XII, 5–7.

Esper, T., 'Military Self-Sufficiency and Weapons Technology in Muscovite Russia', *Slavic Review*, XXVIII/2 (June 1969) 185–208

Fennell, J.L., *The Emergence of Moscow, 1304–1359* (London 1968)

Fennell, J.L., *The Crisis of Medieval Russia, 1200–1304* (London 1983).

Fennell, J.L., 'The Tver Uprising of 1327: A Study of the Sources', *Jahbücher für Geschichte Osteuropas*, XV (1967) 161–179

Grekov, I.B., & F.F. Shachmagonov, *Mir Istorie; Russkie Zemli v XIII–XV vv. ('The Peace of History; The Russian Lands in the III–XV Centuries')*, in Russian (Moscow 1988)

Gorelik, M.V., 'Kulikovskaya Bitva 1380. Russki i Zolotoordinski Voini' ('The Battle of Kulikovskaya 1380. Russian and Golden Horde Warriors)', *Zeughaus* I (1992), 2–7

Gorelik, M.V., 'Mongolo-Tatarskoe Zashitnoe Vooryzhenie Vtoroy Polovini XIV–Nachala XV vv.' ('Mongol-Tatar Defensive Armament of the Second Half of the XIVth to the Early XVth Centuries'), in *Kulikovskaya Bitva v Istorie i Kulture Nashey Rodini ('The Battle of Kulikova in the History and Culture of our Motherland')*, in Russian (Moscow 1983), 238–269

Gorelik, M.V., 'Oruzhye Vorsklinskoy Bitvi' ('Weapons of the Battle of Vorskla') in Russian, *Zeughaus* III (1994), 21–25

Gumilev, L.N., 'Les Mongoles de XIIIe siècle et la Slovo o polku Igoreve', *Cahiers du monde russe et soviétique*, VII/1 (January–March 1966) 37–57

Halperin, C.J., 'The Concept of the *ruskaia zemlia* and Medieval National Consciousness from the Tenth to the Fifteenth Centuries', *Nationalities Papers*, VIII/1 (Spring 1980) 75–86

Halperin, C.J., 'Know Thy Enemy: Medieval Russian Familiarity with the Mongols of the Golden Horde', *Jahbücher für Geschichte Osteuropas*, XXX (1982) 161–173

Halperin, C.J., *Russia and the Golden Horde* (London 1985)

Halperin, C.J., 'Russia and the Mongol Empire in Comparative

A man with a characteristic medieval Russian hat and carrying a substantial crescent-bladed axe or *berdish*, between a group of priests and an apparent group of citizens. *History of Novgorod*, Russian manuscript, 15th C. (Kremlin Museum, Novgorod)

The **Water-Raising Tower** at one corner of the most famous of all Russian *kremlins* or citadels – that of Moscow. Designed by an Italian architect, Pietro Antonio, it was built around 1490. (D.Nicolle photograph)

Perspective', *Harvard Journal of Asian Studies,* XLIII/1 (June 1983) 239–261

Halperin, C.J., 'The Russian Land and the Russia Tsar: The Emergence of Muscovite Ideology, 1380–1408', *Forschungen zur osteuropaischen Geschichte,* XXIII (1976) 7–103

Halperin, C.J., 'Tsarev ulus: Russia in the Golden Horde', *Cahiers du monde russe et soviétique,* XXIII/2 (April–June 1982) 257–263

Kargalov, V.V., *Sverjenie Mongolo-Tatarskogo Iga ('The Overthrow of the Mongol-Tatar Yoke'),* in Russian (Moscow 1973)

Kargalov, V.V., & A.N.Sacharov, *Polkovodsi Drevniye Rusi ('Military Leaders of Ancient Rus'),* in Russian (Moscow 1985)

Kirpichnikov, A.N., *Drevnerusskoe Oruzhye ('Ancient Russian Arms'),* in Russian (Leningrad 1971)

Kirpichnikov, A.N., *Voennoye Delo na Rusi v XII–XV vv. ('Russian Military Affairs in the XII–XV Centuries'),* in Russian (Leningrad 1976)

Kirpichnikov, A.N., & A.F. Medvedev, *Vooruzhenie. Drevniaya Rus: Gorod, Zamok, Sel ('Armament. Ancient Rus: Town, Castle, Village'),* in Russian (Moscow 1985)

Kollmann, N.S., *Kinship and Politics: The Origin and Evolution of the Muscovite Boyar Élite in the Fifteenth Century,* (Dissertation, Harvard University 1980)

Kradin, N.P., *Russkoe Derevjannoe Zodchestvo ('Russian Wooden Defensive Architecture'),* in Russian (Moscow 1988)

Langer, L.N., 'The Medieval Russian Town', in M. Hamm (ed.), *The City in Russian History* (Lexington, Kentucky 1976) 11–33

Makovskaya, L.K., *Ruchnoye Ognestrelnoe Oryzhya Russkoy Armee Kontsa XIV–XVIII vv. ('Handheld Firearms of the Russian Army from the end of the XIV to the XVIII Centuries')* in Russian (Moscow 1992)

Medvedev, A.F., *K Istorie Plastinchatogo Dospecha na Rusi ('The History of Plate Armour in Russia')* in Russian, *Soviet Archaeology* 2 (Moscow 1959)

Miller, Y., (ed.), *Russian Arms and Armour* (Leningrad 1982)

Noonan, T.S., 'Medieval Russia, the Mongols and the West: Novgorod's Relations with the Baltic, 1100–1350', *Medieval Studies,* XXXVII (1975) 316–339

Pelenski, J., *Russia and Kazan. Conquest and Imperial Ideology 1438–1560* (The Hague 1973)

Spuler, B., *Die Goldene Horde. Die Mongolen in Russland 1223–1502* (Wiesbaden 1965)

Toroptsev, A., *Ot Rusi k Rossii: Kievskaya Rusi ('From Rusi to Russia: Kievan Rus'),* in Russian (Moscow 2000)

Vernadsky, G., *The Mongols of Russia* (New Haven 1953)

THE PLATES

A: CAVALRY, 1250–1300

A1: Western Russian cavalryman, fully armoured
This horseman's arms and armour illustrate the mixture of military influences seen in western Russia during this period. The helmet is a type also seem as far away as the Byzantine Empire and the Balkans, while his 'grooved' or 'keeled' shield is of the so-called 'small Lithuanian pavise' type. He is armed with a spear and javelins rather than spear and bow, indicating that Lithuanian light cavalry influence was stronger than that of the otherwise dominant Mongol-Tatars. The sword was probably imported from central Europe.

A2: Boyar nobleman from Pskov
The high-ranking soldier seen here in the process of putting on his armour as yet wears only mail chausses, of basically European form. While his massive and decorated sword is again probably of German origin, his helmet – with a metallic icon on the front, and an eye-piece plus nasal somewhat resembling a pair of spectacles, as well as a long face-covering mail aventail – is clearly within a long-established Russian or even Near Asian tradition.

A3: South-Eastern Russian cavalryman
This fully armoured horse-archer, from that part of Russia most exposed to Turco-Mongol military influence from the steppes, has the abundant military equipment long associated with the military élites of these regions. He does not, however, wear lamellar or any form of armour other than a simple short-sleeved mail hauberk. His archery equipment and curved sabre are similar to those seen across south-eastern Europe, much of the Middle East and as far away as Central Asia. A small hardened leather wrist-protecting bracer was often worn on the lower left arm.

B: INFANTRY, 1250–1325

B1: Russian crossbowman
During this period the arms and armour of infantry, perhaps even more than cavalry, reflected the variety of military-technological influences seen in later 13th- and 14th-century Russia. His cross-bow and associated equipment, as well as his short but quite broad sword, are typically Middle European, though rather old-fashioned. The same is true of his mail hauberk and the quilted garment beneath it. But his tall, pointed, narrow-brimmed helmet is distinctly Russian, as are the boots which might indicate that he would normally expect to be riding a horse as a mounted infantryman.

B2: Urban militiaman
Once again we see high boots of soft, and in this case slightly decorated leather. Such footwear was, of course, necessary in the fierce Russian winters and in the typically muddy seasons of early spring and late autumn. Whereas the substantial sword, broad-bladed infantry spear and large shield carried by this militiaman – and indeed his full armour – are comparable to those seen among the best-equipped urban troops across Europe, the actual structure of the armour is distinctive. The helmet of directly riveted iron segments is within a long-established Russian tradition and has been given a thickly quilted Mongol-style aventail instead of the mail aventail normally seen elsewhere in Europe. His massive, scale-lined, fabric-covered cuirass with its large arm-flaps is also unlike anything normally seen in other parts of Europe, and again probably reflects Mongol influence.

B3: Light infantry archer
Unlike his companions, this foot soldier represents an entirely Russian tradition which owed little to outside influences. His hat and footwear mark him out as an ordinary man, if not necessarily a peasant. His thickly quilted coat with its very tall collar protects him from the weather as well as offering some protection against blows. His large infantry bow of semi-composite construction was not, of course, confined to Russia, being of a type seen across the northernmost parts of Europe and Asia as well as in the pre-Turkish Middle East. His axe may reflect a shared military heritage with Scandinavia; and only the decorated quiver on his right hip might betray some Turco-Mongol influence, though even this was probably within a tradition which Russia shared with the rest of northern Asia.

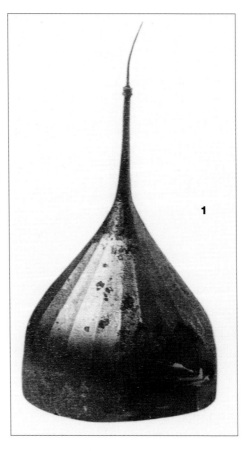

C: CAVALRY, 1300–75

C1: Western Russian light cavalryman, c.1350
During the 14th century the difference in arms, armour and overall military styles increased between the western and eastern regions of Russia, and several western principalities began to fall under Lithuanian, and subsequently combined Polish-Lithuanian control. Nevertheless

this cavalryman is still distinguished by his use of a lamellar cuirass in addition to ordinary central European mail armour. His sword is a curved sabre, which was not used much further west, while his shield with its vertical 'keel' is a development of the Lithuanian pavise.

C2: Western Russian heavy cavalryman, c.1375
This member of the western Russian military elite has adopted the plated iron arm and leg protections which were characteristic of the knightly cavalryman in the rest of Europe. Only his helmet, which would have been considered old-fashioned in Germany or France, and his scale cuirass, which betrays Mongol influence, set him apart from the heavily armoured cavalrymen seen further west. His horse is, however, protected by a plated chamfron and lamellar horse-armour which came straight from the Turco-Mongol steppe tradition.

C3: Novgorod urban cavalryman, c.1350
Paradoxically this armoured horse-archer from the north-western Russian state of Novgorod is equipped in a remarkably Turco-Mongol or even Islamic style. Nothing about his arms, armour and horse harness shows European influence; even the decoration of the flaps of lamellar armour which protect his upper arms, and the scale-lined body armour which he wears beneath a sleeveless tunic, are virtually identical to the armour seen within the Mongol Golden Horde and in Islamic Transoxania. Such styles almost certainly stemmed from these eastern territories. The fighting dog which tries to defend its endangered master does, however, seem to have been a typically Russian or Turco-Mongol phenomenon.

D: INFANTRY, 1325–1400
D1: Dismounted nobleman, mid-14th century
During the 14th century a distinctively Russian style of arms and armour re-emerged. It combined several traditions, though of course Mongol influence remained strong. During the 14th and 15th centuries Russian arms, armour, horse-harness and general military costume diverged sharply from that of the rest of Europe, remaining highly distinctive until the reign of Peter the Great. Here, for example, a noble warrior has both mail and lamellar armour, plus a helmet which would not have been out of place in the Middle East. But his sword is Western European, as is his shield, though the latter would now be considered old-fashioned further west.

D2: Infantryman from Suzdal, mid-14th century
Separated from the western or European frontiers of Russia by huge distances and several rival states, most of which were under the same Mongol overlordship which had been imposed on Suzdal, it is not surprising that this infantryman's equipment looks rather archaic. On the other hand it also reflects virtually no Turco-Mongol influence. As such it is probably a continuation of an old but now isolated military tradition.

D3: Crossbowman, late 14th century
In contrast to the preceding figure, this crossbowman combines distinctively Russian clothing and armour, including a thickly quilted coat beneath a cuirass of embossed scales, with a Western European sword and typical European crossbow equipment. Meanwhile his helmet seems to represent a continuation of a specifically Russian military tradition.

E: EASTERN RUSSIA, 1375–1425
E1: Cavalryman, late 14th century
During the later 14th and 15th centuries a new power arose within the array of Russian principalities. This was Moscow, or Muscovy, and its increasingly effective armies were largely based upon a Russian version of Mongol military traditions, including arms and armour as well as organisation and tactics. As in Mongol armies, there was a large and formidable élite of heavily armoured cavalrymen. As illustrated here, they largely relied upon Turco-Mongol forms of lamellar and other armours, but also made use of various pieces of Western European-type equipment such as this man's knee protections; whether the latter were made locally or were imported from elsewhere in Europe is, however, unknown.

E2: Mounted drummer, early 15th century
The importance of drums, often carried on horseback, in the control and motivation of Muscovite armies was another obvious example of Mongol military influence. In fact the role of mounted drummers placed late medieval Muscovy within a military tradition that extended across a vast area from the borders of China to the Islamic world and Granada in

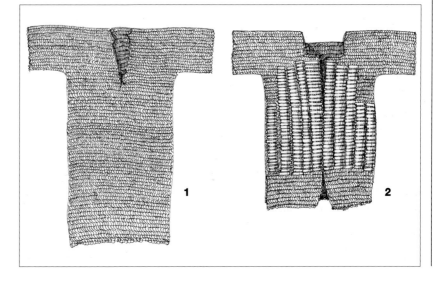

OPPOSITE **Late medieval Russian helmets.**
(1) Fluted helmet of 14th–15th Cs (National Historical Museum, Moscow)
(2) 15th-C northern Russian helmet of a type which could be seen right across Russia and also in Iran. (Kremlin Museum, Novgorod)

RIGHT **Russian armour.**
(1) A short-sleeved mail hauberk found at the site of the battle of Kulikovo Field, 1380.
(2) A mail-and-plate *bekhterets* of the late 15th or 16th C. (Drawings by A.S. Sheps)

LEFT **Late medieval Russian mail hauberk found at the site of the battle of Kulikovo Field, 1380. (Battlefield Site Museum, Kulikovo)**

RIGHT **Fragment of scale armour from a Russian cuirass, perhaps from the 14th C. (Kremlin Museum, Novgorod)**

southern Spain. This man's armour is so typical of western Asia that it could well have been manufactured in Iran or the Caucasus. His helmet, consisting of a mail hood reinforced with iron plates, similarly recalls the distinctive *zirih-kulah* protections of the Caucasus.

E3: Prince in gilded armour, late 14th century
Although this figure seems to combine the military traditions of East and West, his armour is nevertheless very similar to that seen across the Golden Horde and even into Transoxania and Iran. This includes his plated arm defences, scale-covered gauntlets and metallic greaves. Meanwhile his splendidly gilded armour incorporates a simple helmet with an anthropomorphic visor which might hark back to pre-Mongol Turkish peoples of the western steppes. Typically, perhaps, the armour of his horse is entirely within the Turco-Mongol western Asiatic tradition, since this was a field in which Europe had little to offer.

F: WESTERN RUSSIA & 'GREAT LITHUANIA', 15TH CENTURY

F1: Heavy cavalryman, early 15th century
During the 15th century the western half or more of what had been medieval Russia disappeared as a separate entity, to be incorporated into what was for a short time the biggest territorial state in Europe – the combined Kingdom and Grand Duchy of Poland-Lithuania. The Russian-speaking territories fell within the Lithuanian part of this remarkable state; and as the Lithuanians were themselves few in number, the state and its armies became to a substantial extent Russian. Nevertheless the arms and armour used by its heavily armoured cavalry élite were clearly within the Western European military-technological tradition. Only the horse harness and the man's shield – which was of a type also seen across the Balkans, in Hungary and Poland – distinguishes him from an early 15th-century Italian professional cavalryman.

F2: Novgorod noble cavalryman, mid-15th century
Few of the figures reconstructed in this book combine the traditions of East and West to the same degree as this nobleman. His helmet, mail aventail, and the light but effective mail-and-plate cuirass which he wears over his mail hauberk are very Russian. The same could be said of his heavy fur-lined cloak; but the full plate armour defences for his arms and legs must surely have been imported from Germany or even Italy. Unlike that of most Russian cavalry, his horse harness is more European than Turco-Mongol.

F3: Infantryman, late 15th century
The main feature to note about this fully armoured infantryman is that, outside Russia, his mail and quilted body armour would have seemed more typical of the 14th or even 13th centuries than of the 15th. The most modern item is his helmet, of Italian origin and perhaps imported via the Italian trading outposts on the Black Sea coast. On the other hand his mace, axe, and substantial pavise shield are very up-to-date.

G: MUSCOVITE FIELD ARMIES, 1425–1500

G1: Cavalryman, early 15th century
One feature which would remain characteristic of Muscovite armoured cavalry for several centuries was their preference for helmets with remarkably tall points. This style may have

originated further east, but it became the hallmark of Muscovite troops not only in their own art but in European representations of Russian horsemen. The rest of this armoured horse-archer's equipment is similar to that of his late Golden Horde Turco-Mongol overlords and foes.

G2: Heavy cavalryman, late 15th century
By the late 15th century Muscovy had become the dominant partner in relation to the fragmenting khanates of what had been the vast Mongol Golden Horde. Muscovite armies were also posing a problem for Poland-Lithuania to the west; in fact, Muscovy had become the powerhouse from which a new and revived Russia soon emerged. This man's helmet, though of an angular form with an interesting multiple mail aventail, still has the preferred high-pointed summit. His armour is of mail and mail-and-plate construction, while his shield is entirely plated with iron segments.

G3: Infantryman, early 15th century
Like the Mongol armies which it gradually replaced, the most important part of the Muscovite army was cavalry; but infantry did play a significant role, even in open field battles. They seem to have included quite heavily armoured spearmen and axemen such as the man shown here. Once again, his equipment mixes the traditions of East and West, Russia, Europe and the Mongol world. His axe and shield would, however, not normally have been seen in the armies of the remaining Mongol khanates.

H: MUSCOVITE GARRISONS, c.1450–1500
H1: Dismounted horse-archer, end of the 15th century
Fast-expanding Muscovy never included as many castles and fortresses as neighbouring European states to the west. Nevertheless, many *kremlins* or urban citadels were gradually provided with stone defences to replace their old wooden ones, and several stone or brick fortresses were constructed in the north-west, west and south-west of the country. These needed to be garrisoned, and so the importance of infantry gradually increased. Although the man shown here is a dismounted cavalryman, the size of his bow suggests that it was designed for use on foot. His 'helmet' is again of a distinctive mail-and-plate construction, as is the upper part of his body armour. The decoratively engraved vambraces on his lower arms are, however, of a type characteristic of the Islamic world and Russia rather than of Western Europe.

H2: Musketeer, mid-15th century
The Russians adopted firearms enthusiastically and there is plenty of evidence to show that guns were soon being manufactured in Muscovy. This man has a heavy hand hold gun of a type which could by now be seen throughout Europe. His costume, including a thickly quilted coat and heavy boots, plus his tall pointed helmet with its ear-flaps and mail aventail, are distinctively Russian.

H3: Dismounted officer, end of the 15th century
It is interesting to note that a type of helmet normally associated with the Ottoman Turks in the Balkans and the Middle East was also seen in Russia, despite the fact that many years would pass before Muscovy and the Ottomans actually clashed on the battlefield. This was the *shishak* with its sliding nasal, substantial ear-pieces and, at a slightly later date, an extended neck protection. The rest of this officer's armour, as well as his weaponry and his metallic shield, also find close parallels amongst the Ottoman Turks. Perhaps this indicates that the best equipped Muscovite military élite shared some military traditions with those Muslim Turks who had succeeded the Greek Orthodox Christian Byzantines on the Bosphorus.

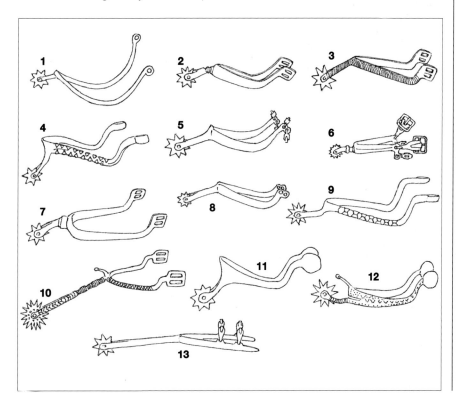

Russian rowel spurs.
(1) From Priozersk, first half of 14th C.
(2) From Staraya Ladoga, 14th C.
(3) From Priozersk, first half of 14th C.
(4) From Novgorod, 14th C.
(5) From Vladimir region, 14th–15th C.
(6) From Priozersk, first half of 14th C.
(7) From St Petersburg region, 14th–15th C.
(8) From Serensk, second half of 14th/ first half of 15th C.
(9) From Kingiseppi, second half of 14th/ first half of 15th C.
(10) From Novgorod, 1420s.
(11) From Novgorod, second half of 15th C.
(12) From Novgorod, 15th C.
(13) From Vishgorod, 15th C.

INDEX

Figures in **bold** refer to illustrations